I0494407

Cute Pets Website

For my husband

Respect

Kitty is happy. She became a new black handy. That was a big surprise 🪼. Now the Cute pets are thinking 😐 about a new Website. Mr. Feiler have a great new site. He found webhosting for free. Since 14 years Mr. and Mrs. Feiler work for a day care in Pet City. They have met amber on a charity event, talked with her about the day care, because amber has such an institution like April Lone, the famous singer. It's time for a new Cute Pets Website...

Naturally with the video of Kitty. The most important point will be: About us. There are all information about the work of Cute Pets.

Responsible for the work of art is X. In the first Saturday Talk at 3 o'clock since a view weeks the theme is Respect: The work of Mr. Feiler. His social engagement for all.

After the discussion about social work and art is the new project, the website. The work of Kitty 🐱 is the eye catcher. After the meeting Kitty makes Images editing for the website and a gallery with Collages.

The pics for the website are ready, also "About us", "Contact", "News", the formalities about Disclaimer and the Links. In the middle of the Site is Kitty 🐱 with the clip. The Name of the Site is The Cute Pets Site. X, Alien 👽, Imhotep and Maehi respect the website of

Mr. Feiler, therefore the extra "DLFV for DLfV". Naturally Kitty talks about the theme with her family, Mr. Feiler says OK 🙇. The chronic is in Work. The Community is working together at the chronic.

That means The Site is ready for the net. Alien 👽 haunts the Site up 👆

This work is done.

The Cute Pets Site

About Us News DLFV for DLfV Links Disclaimer

Kittysong, click here to see the Clip

Contact

Social Network

The best way to see, what is going on, is the Social Network. Therefore the Cute Pets looking for the likes of their Site. One week ago, when the Video Clip of Kitty was in net, the reactions were great. Over thousand Clicks and likes for the Clip. The Cute Pets are sad, that nobody makes a like at their Site. Why? That's normal. X says, it is no reason to be sad, the work goes on. And a view hours later, the likes are coming...

I say Thank you to my husband

www.ingramcontent.com/pod-product-compliance
Lightning Source LLC
Chambersburg PA
CBHW041619180526
45159CB00002BC/933